This journal belongs to:

Anatalica

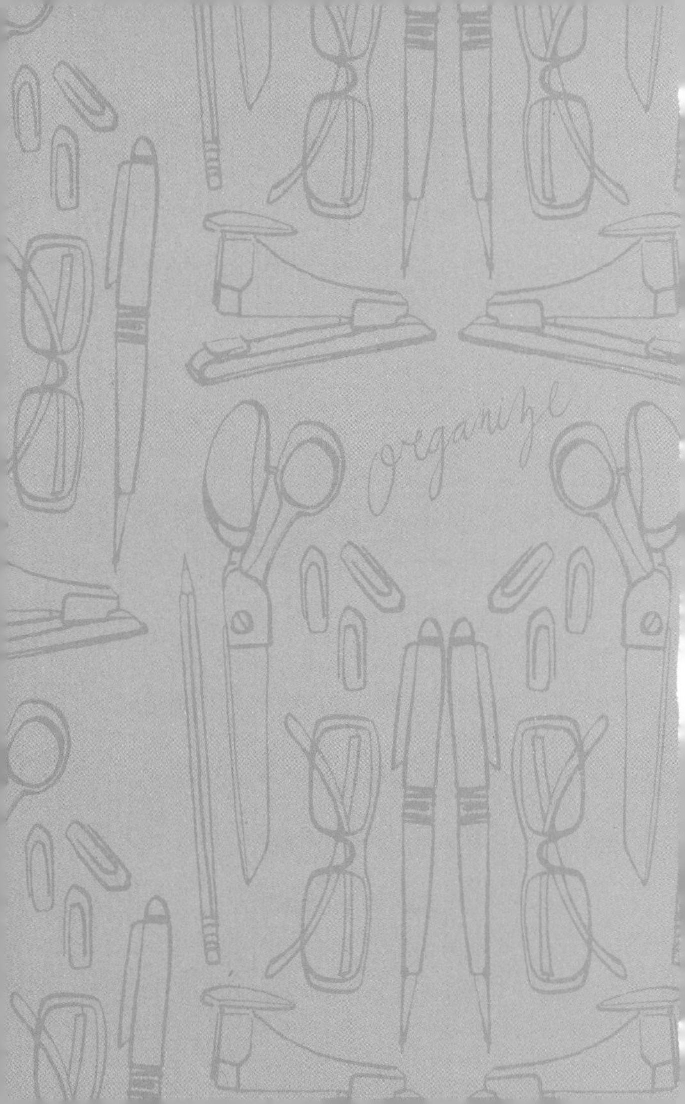
organize

notes

Memo

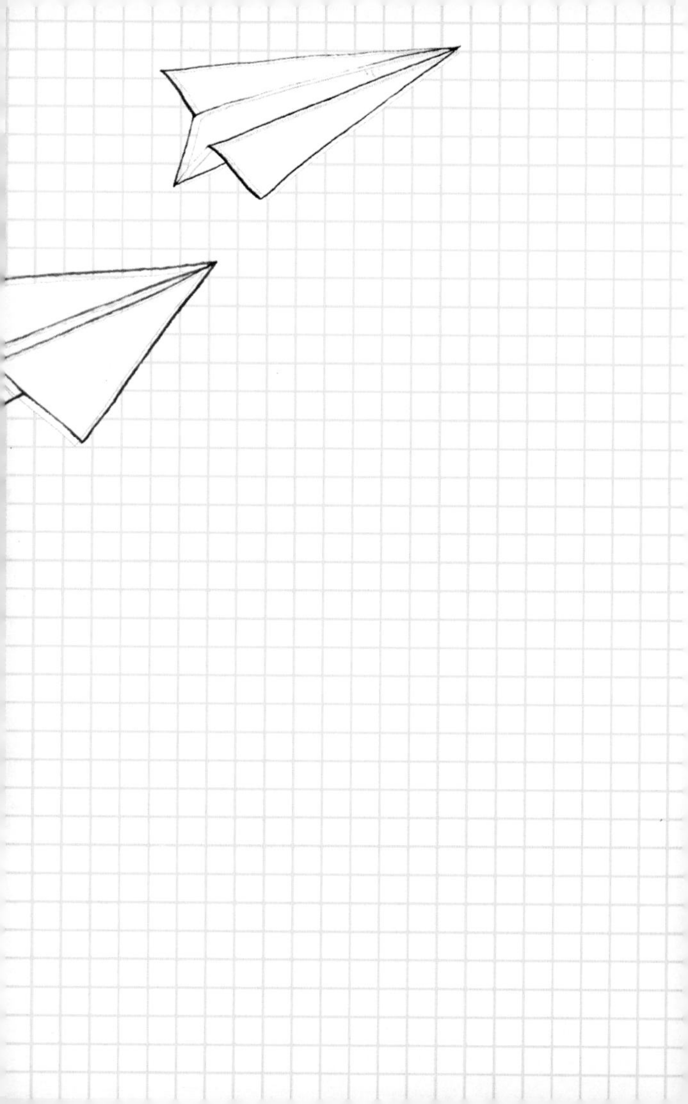

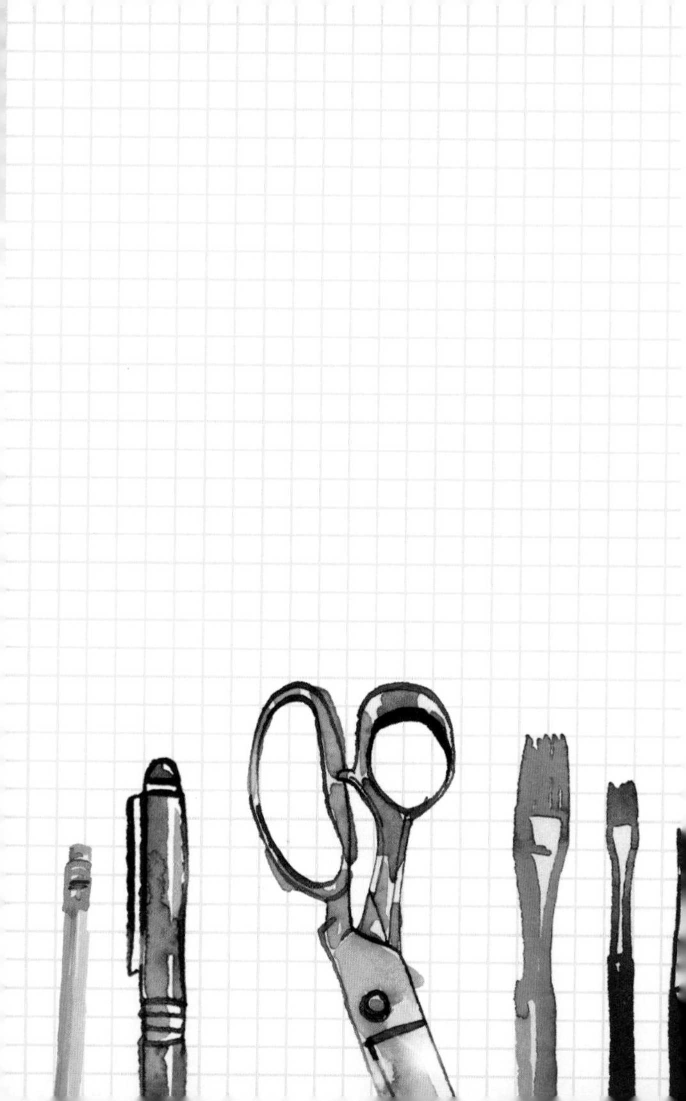

checklist

checklist

great idea

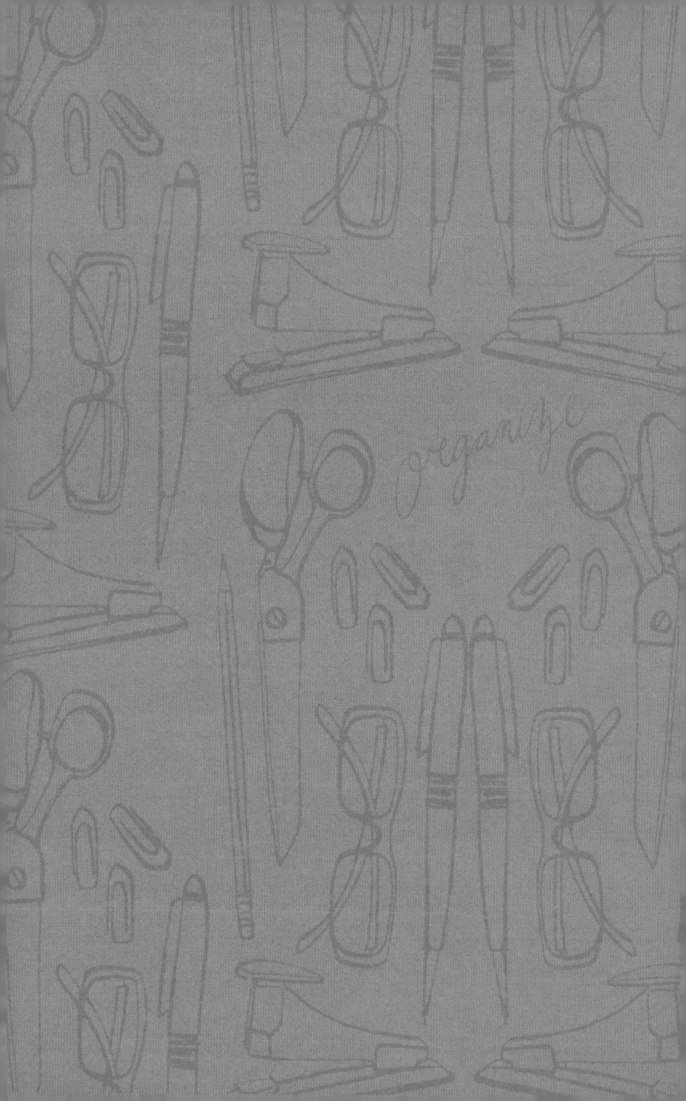
organize

notes

organize

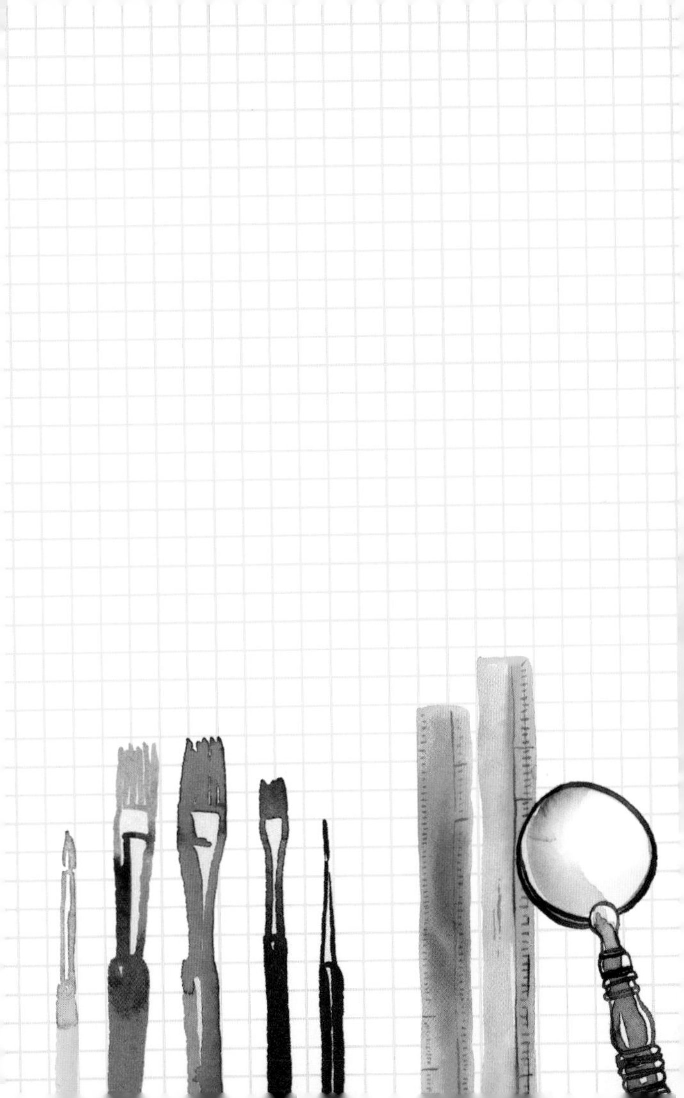

checklist

checklist

great idea

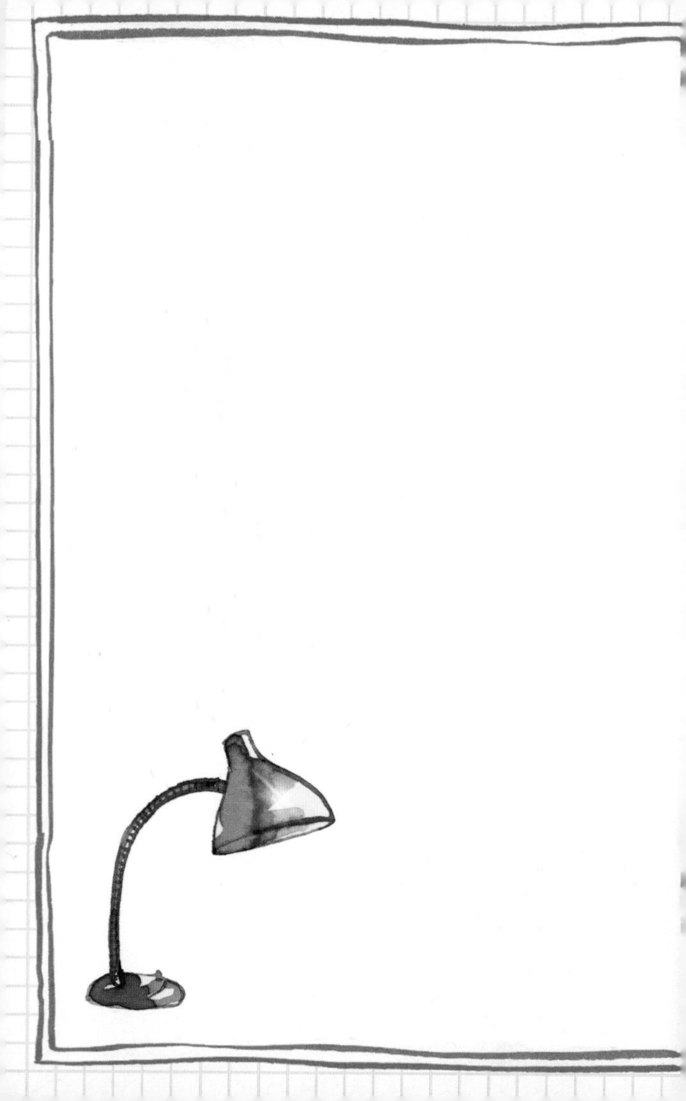

notes

Memo

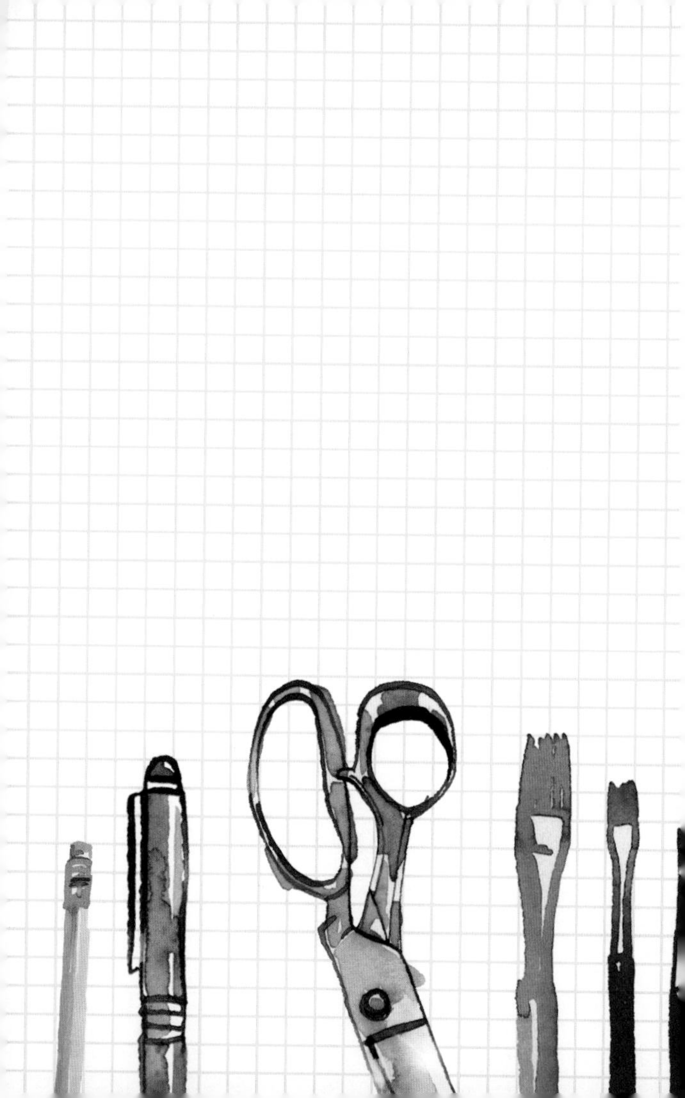

checklist

checklist

great idea

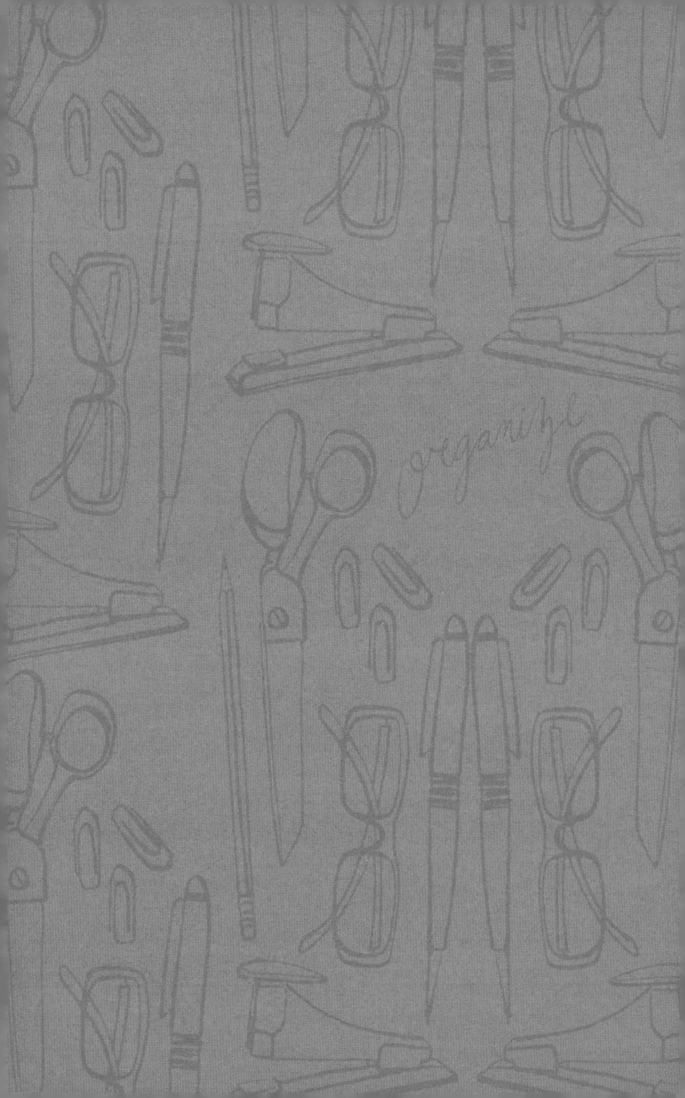
organize

notes

worn in Alaska and the northeastern
2. a long woolen shirt or
hood, worn in Alaska, etc.,
way (pärk'wā'), broad road with
planted with grass, trees, etc.
ey (pär'li), 1. a co[illegible]
talk to discuss ter[illegible]
The general held [illegible]
about exchanging prisoners. 2. dis-
matters, especially with an enemy.
eys, par leyed, par ley ing. countries.
ia ment (pär'lə mənt), a council or
ess that is the highest lawmak[illegible]
in some countri[illegible]

apple. 2. each of several [illegible]
tities into which a whole [illegible]
divided; fraction: A dim[illegible]
part of a dollar. 3. thing that helps
[illegible] whole: A radio ha[illegible]
[illegible] share: He had no [illegible]
[illegible] 5. side in a dispute
[illegible] always takes his brother's pa[illegible]
6. character in a play; the words spoken
a character: Anna spoke the part of
heroine in our play. 7. divide into two
more pieces [illegible]

a play; the word[illegible]
Anna spoke [illegible] part of the
play. 7. divide into two or
8. force apart; divide: The
horseback parted the crowd.
part[illegible]: The friends parted
dividing line left in comb[illegible]
one of the voices or in[illegible]
The four parts in [illegible]
tenor and bass [illegible]

4. leave (an automobile, etc.) for a
a certain place: Park your car here.
to leave an automobile, etc. for [illegible]

organize

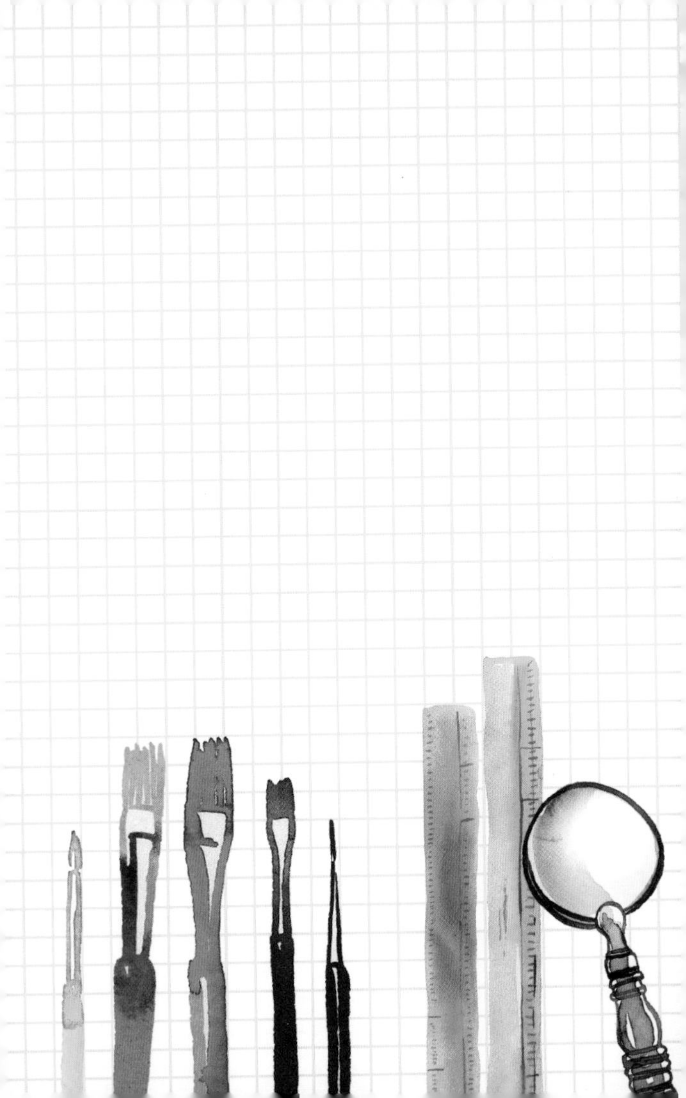

checklist

checklist

great idea

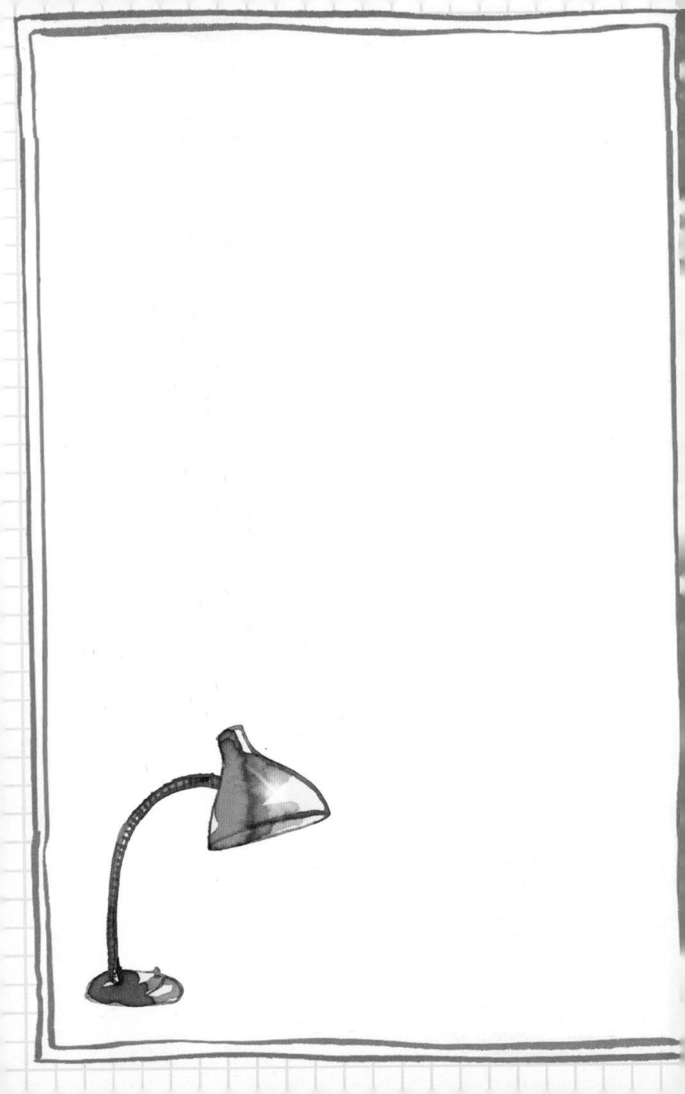

notes

Memo

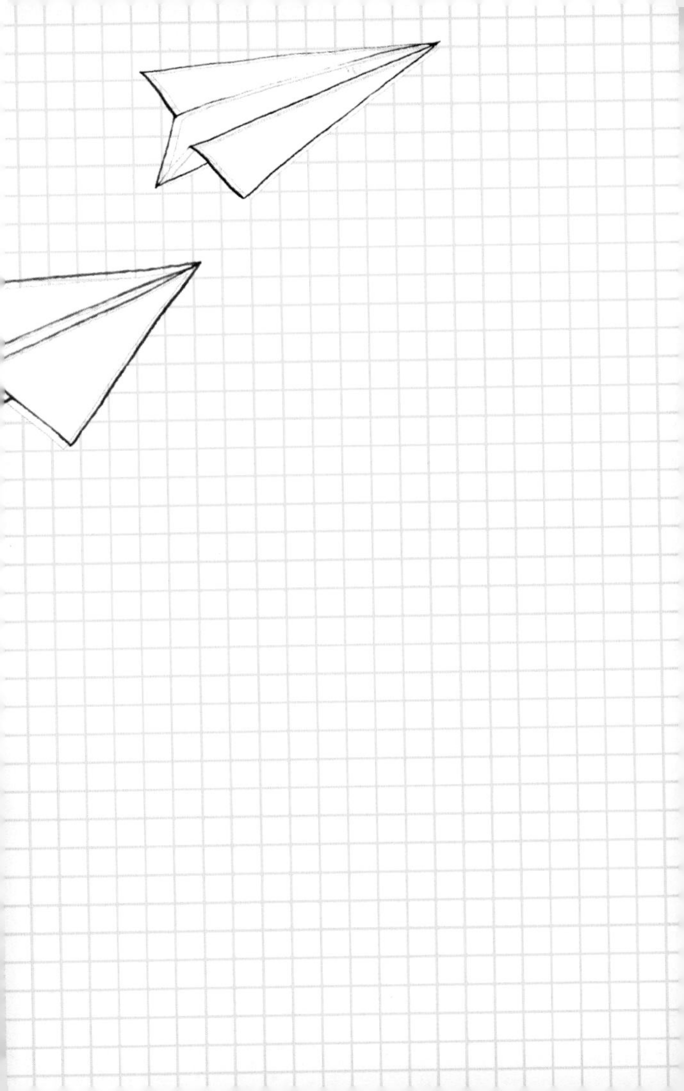

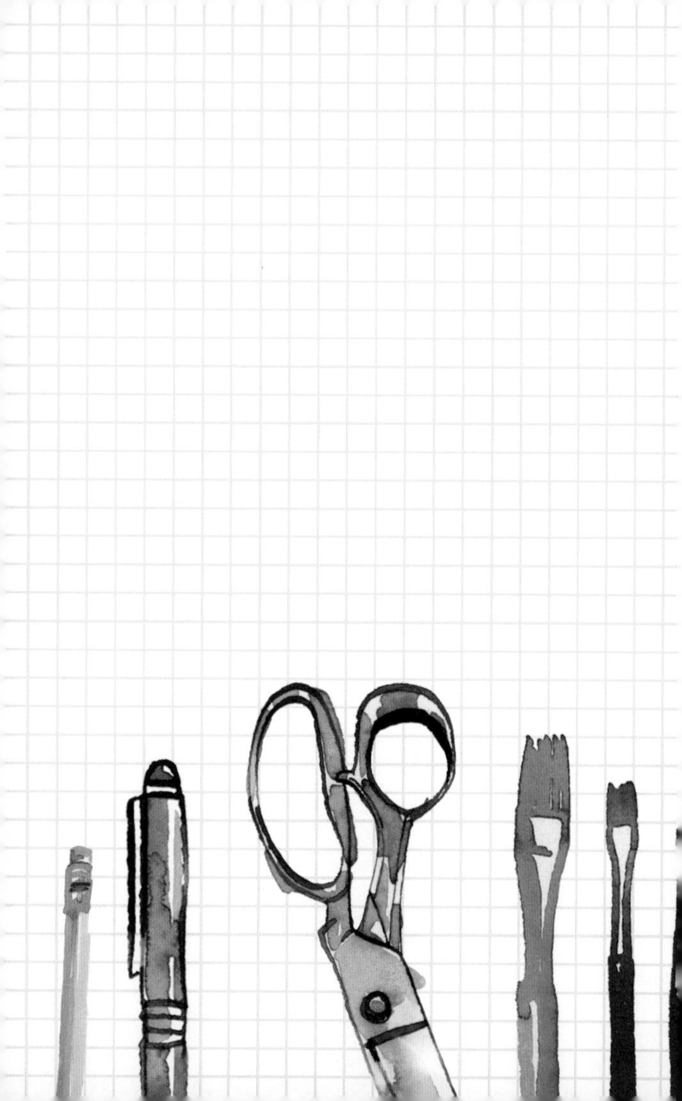

checklist

checklist

great idea

organize

notes

organize

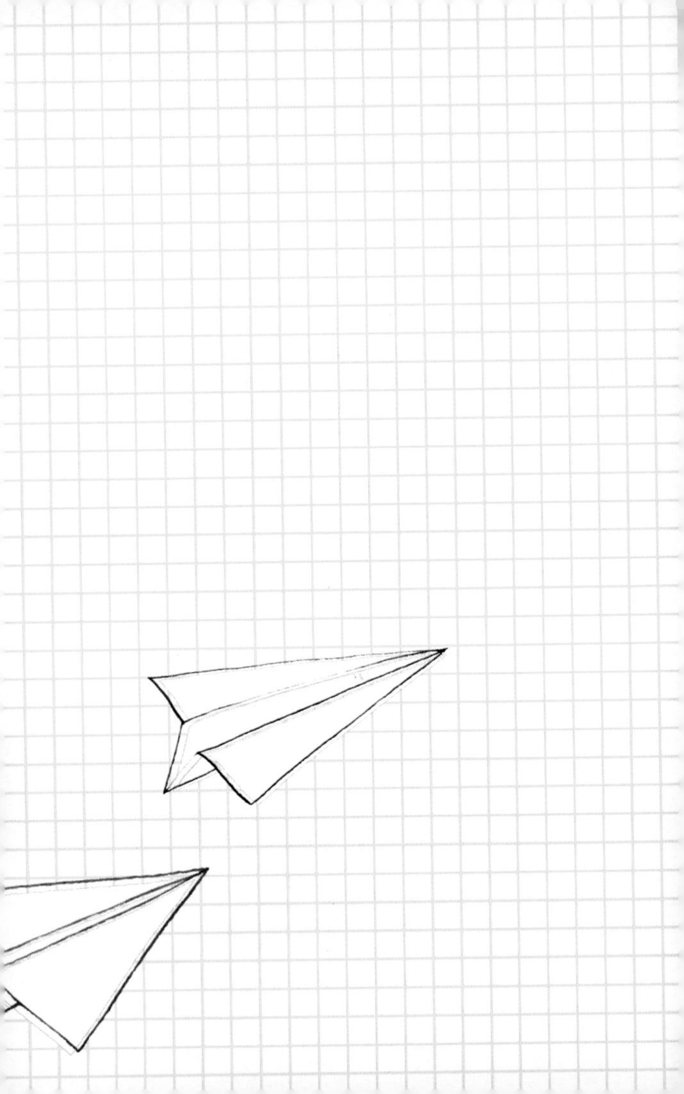

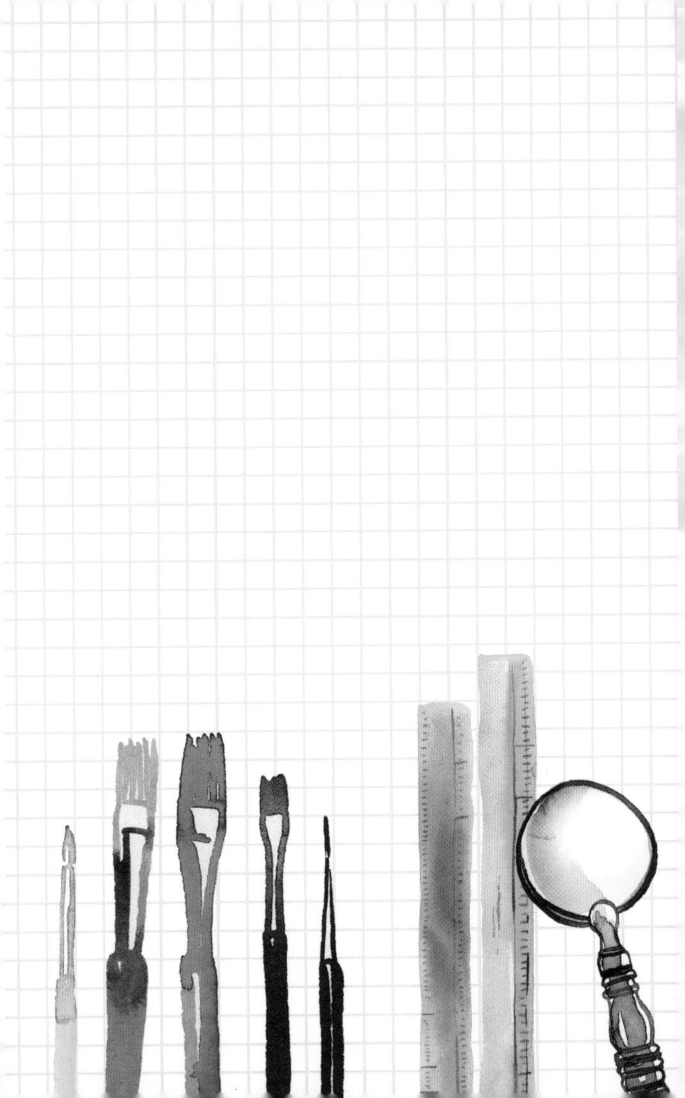

checklist

checklist

great idea

US 7¢
US 7¢

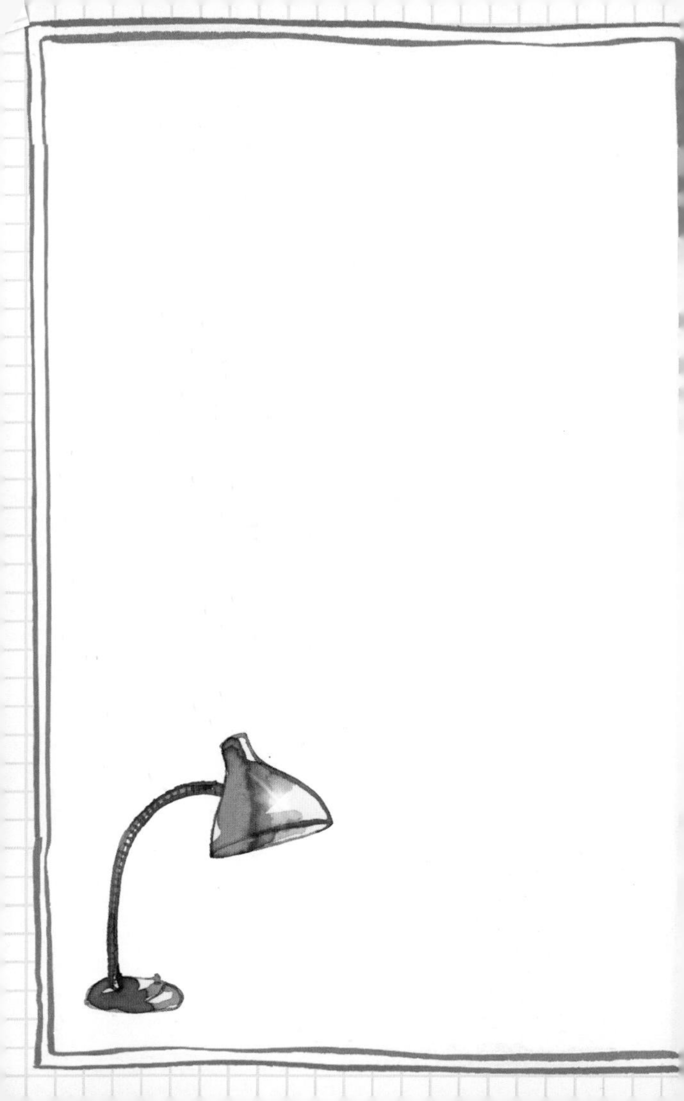

notes

Memo

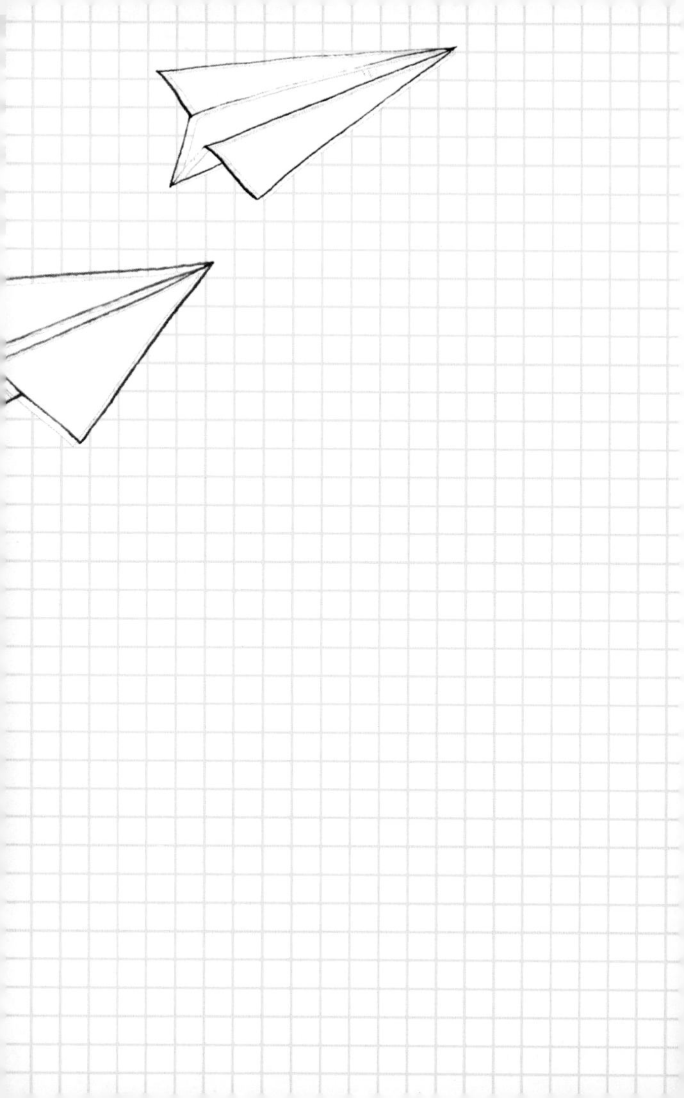

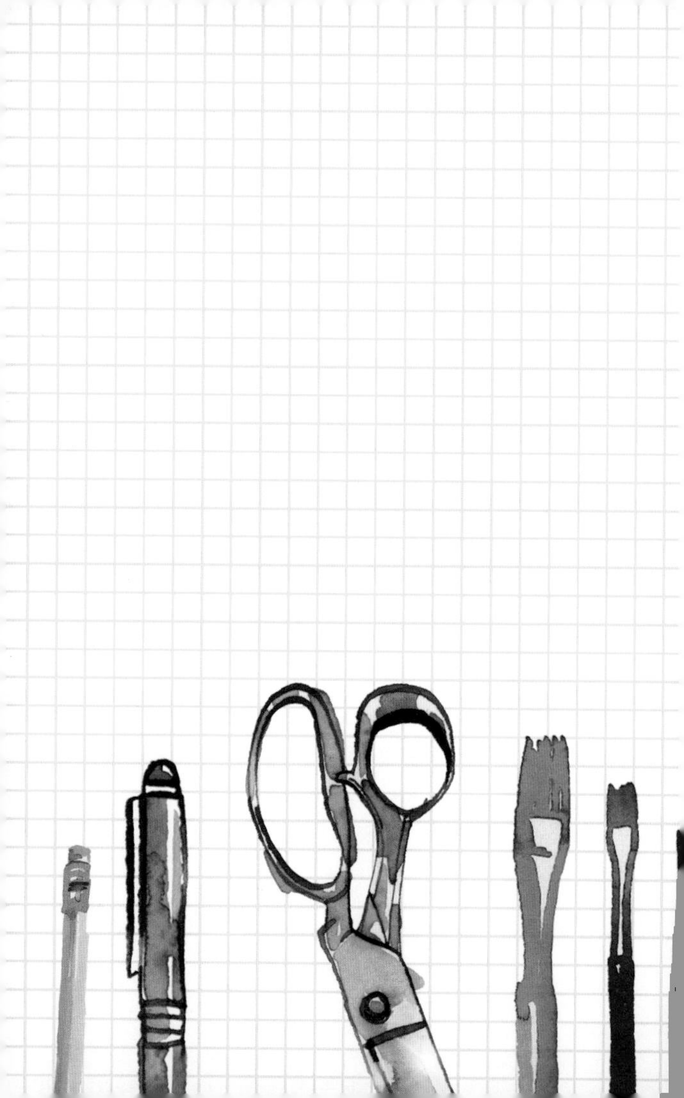

checklist

checklist

great idea

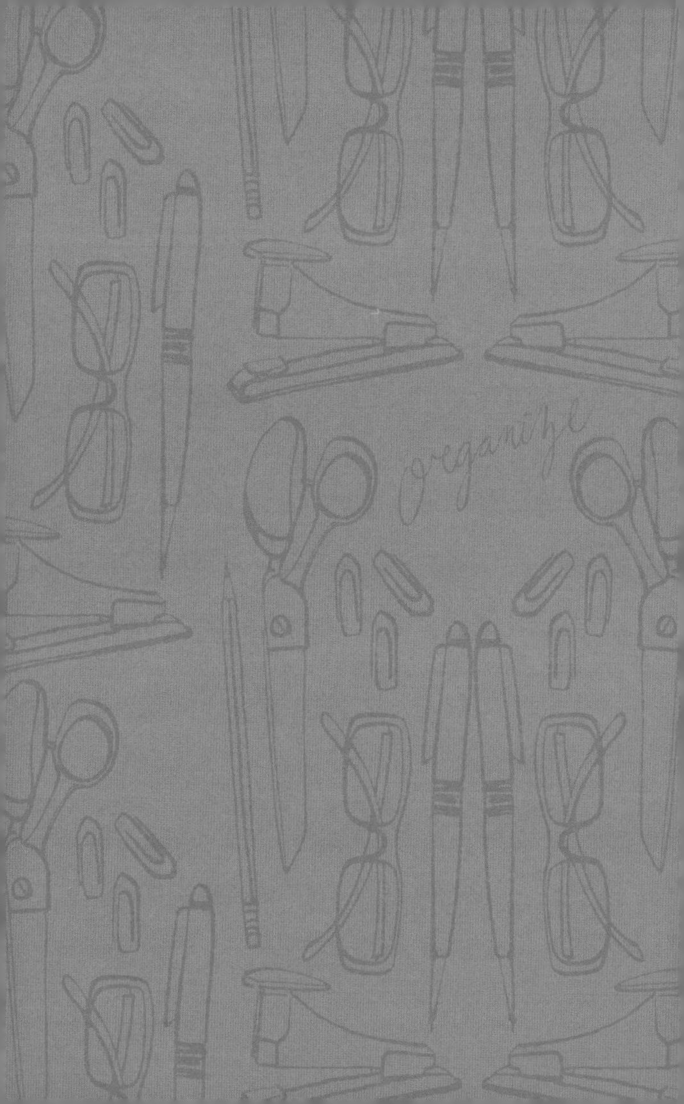
organize

notes

worn in Alaska and the northeastern ... 2. a long woolen shirt or ... hood, worn in Alaska, etc. ... way (pärk′wā′), broad road with ... es planted with grass, trees, etc. ... ley (pär′li), 1. a co[illegible] ... talk to discuss ter[illegible] ... The general held a [illegible] ... about exchanging prisoners. 2. dis- ... matters, especially with an enemy. ... leys, par leyed, par ley ing. countries. ... lia ment (pär′lə mənt), a council or ... gress that is the highest lawmak[illegible] ... in some countries.

apple. 2. each of several equal quan- ... tities into which a whole [illegible] ... divided; fraction: A dime is a tenth ... part of a dollar. 3. thing that helps ... make up a whole: A radio ha[illegible] ... share: He has no ... 5. side in a disput[illegible] ... always takes his brother's p[illegible] ... 6. character in a play; the words spoken ... a character: Anna spoke the part of ... heroine in our play. 7. divide into two ... more pieces

... left in comb ... voices or ... parts in ... d bass. ... a play; the ... Anna spoke ... play. 7. di ... force apa[illegible] ... and set ... and set a ... around ... fur ... and the

... Anna spoke the part of the ... play. 7. divide into two or ... 8. force apart; divide: The ... horseback parted the crowds. ... parate: The friends parted ... viding line left in comb[illegible] ... one of the voices or in[illegible] ... The four parts in ... tenor and bass

... park ... pleas[illegible] ... animals ... 4. leave (an automobile, etc.) for a ... a certain place: Park your car here.

Organize

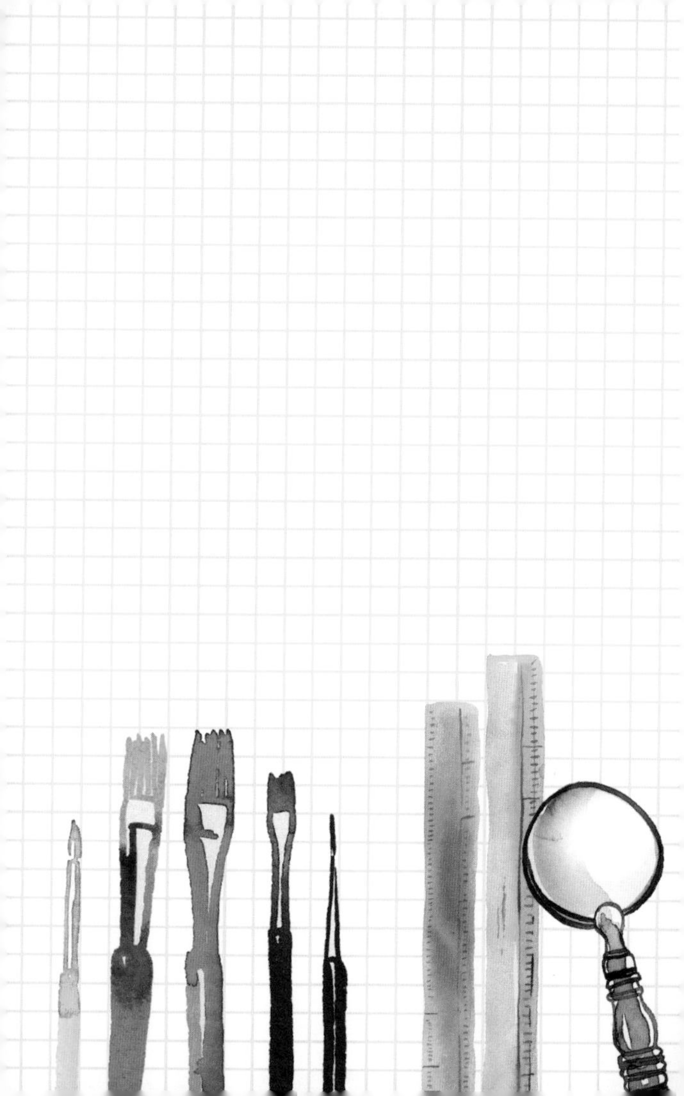

checklist

checklist

great idea

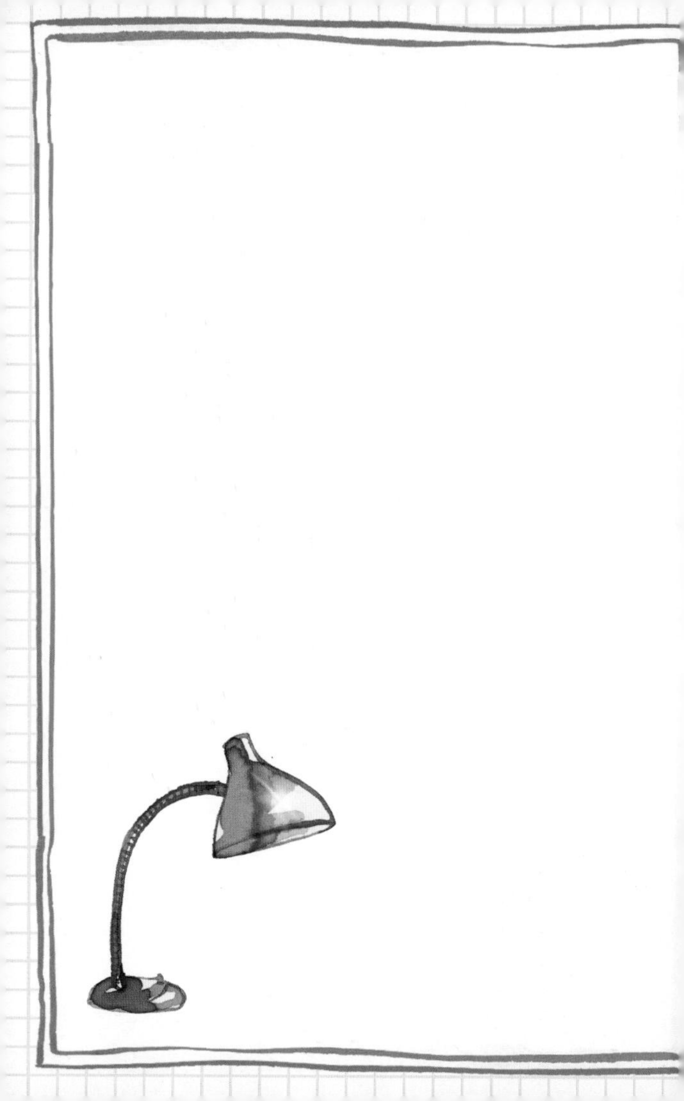

notes

Memo

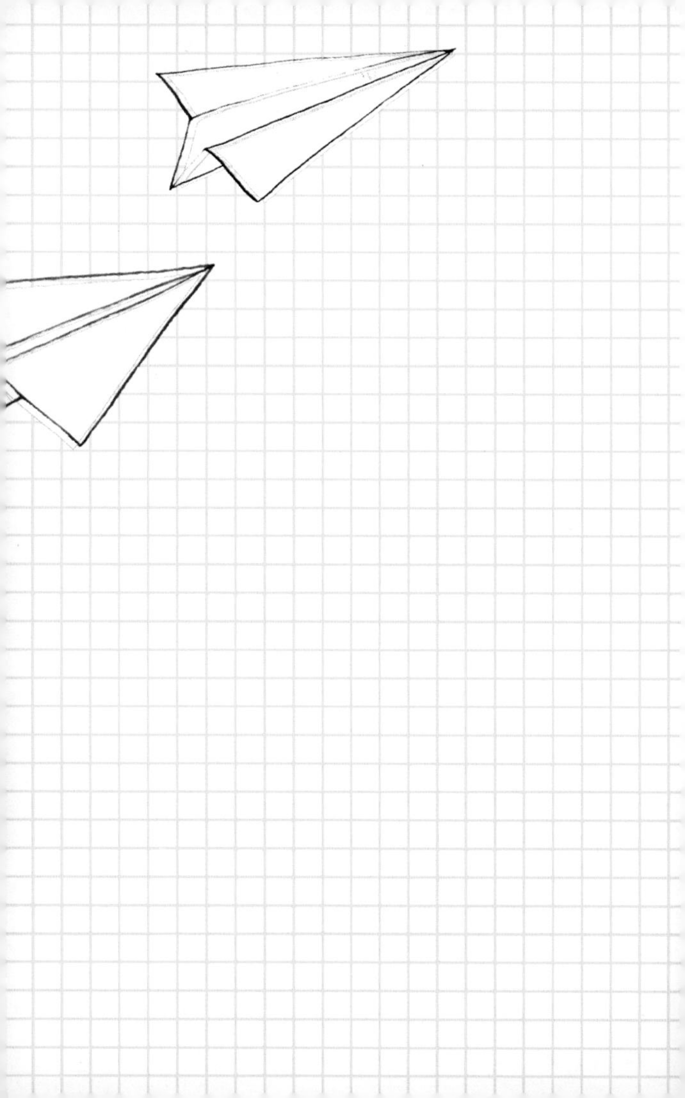

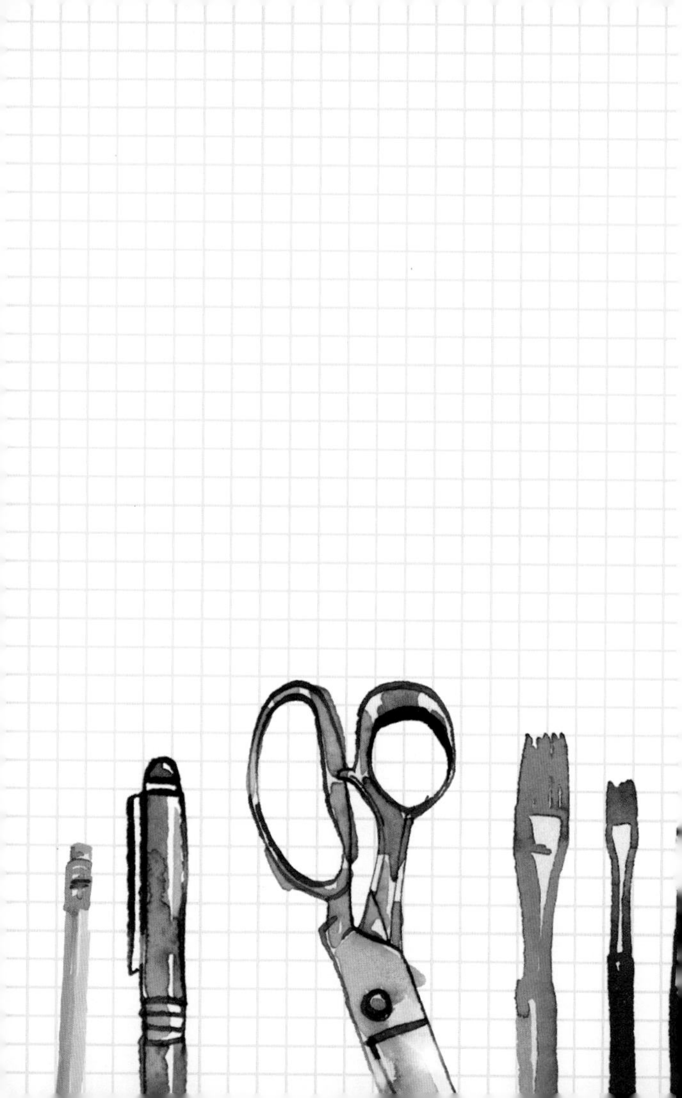

checklist

checklist

great idea

organize

notes

Organize

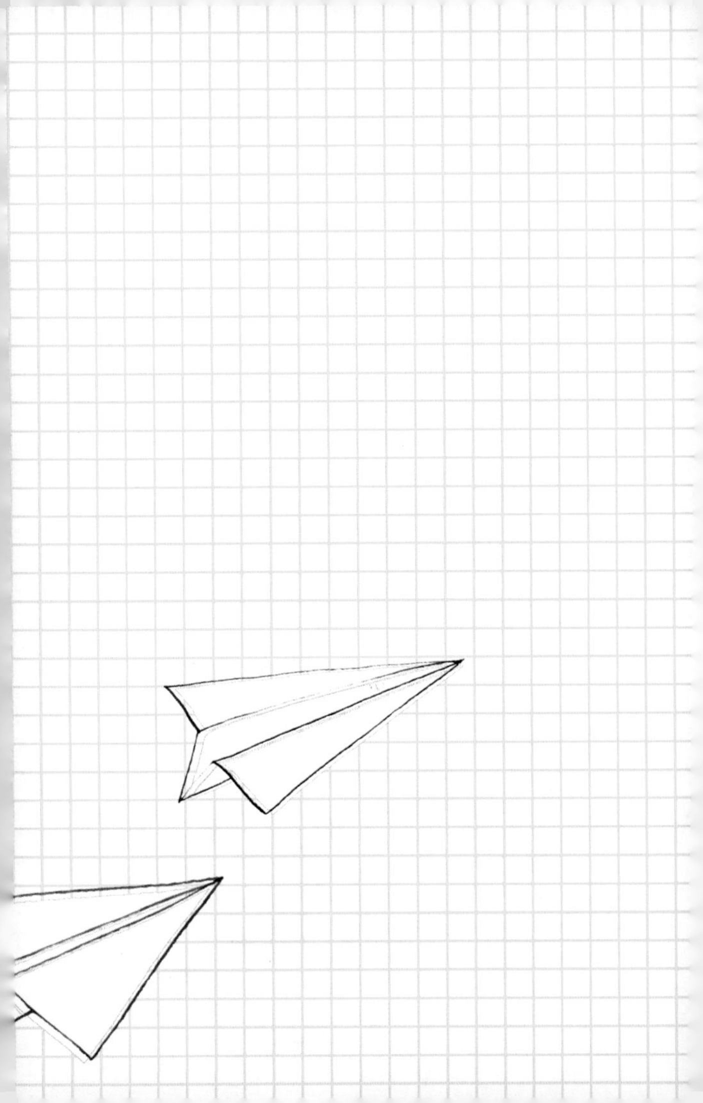

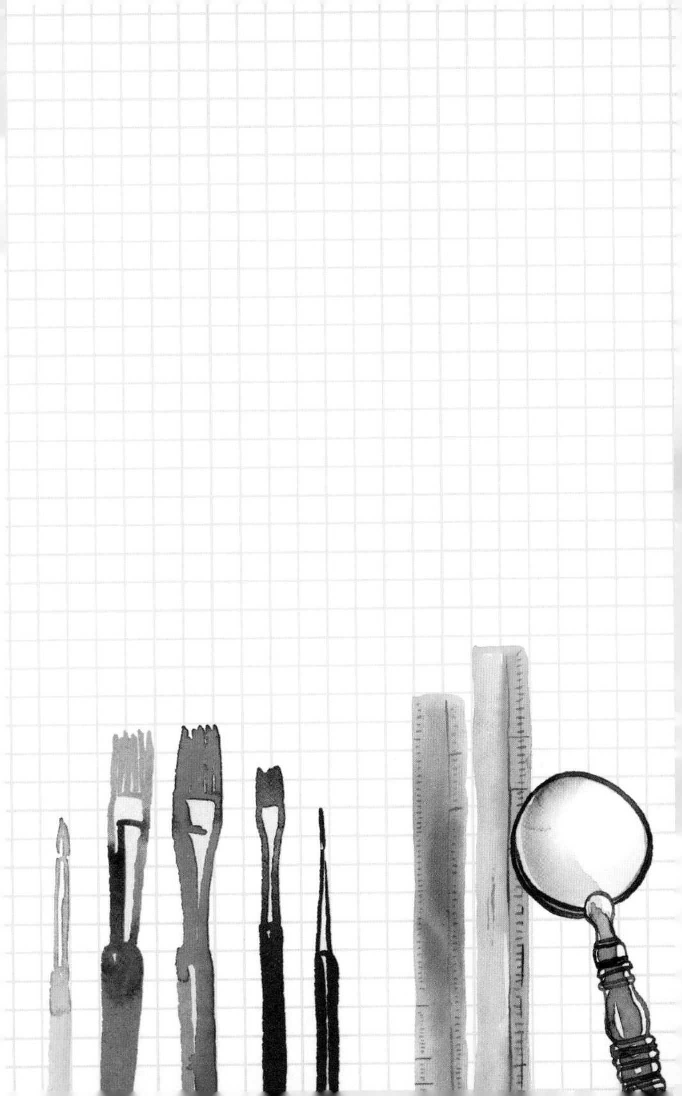

checklist

checklist

great idea

US
US

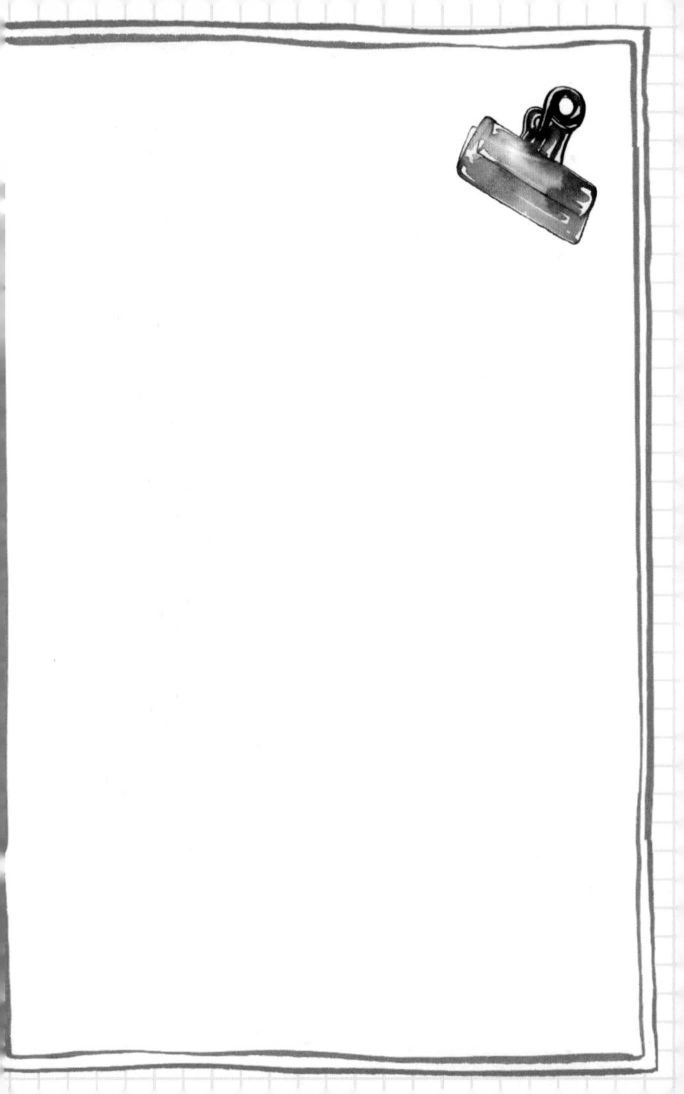

M060616C
ISBN 978-0-7353-3690-2
9 780735 336902

GALISON 28 WEST 44TH STREET · NEW YORK, NY 10036
Designed in the U.S.A. Manufactured in China